The Economic

nd

of

gy

eft

rtouzos

Larson

Ebener

...pared for the
International Electronics Security Group
and the American Electronics Association

Science and Techology Program

RAND

This study examines the costs and implications of hardware thefts for U.S. high-technology firms, focusing on manufacturers and distributors of computers, semiconductors, hard disk drives, and cellular telephones. The report is likely to be of interest to high-technology managers, security professionals, policymakers, and law enforcement officials.

CONTENTS

FIGURES

TABLES

OVERVIEW

Many high-technology hardware products are attractive targets of opportunity for thieves. Although some observers of the high-tech electronics industry believe that thefts of such products are significant, empirical evidence indicating the magnitude of the problem has been lacking.

The International Electronics Security Group (IESG), a consortium of high-technology electronics industry security executives from the computer, semiconductor, hard disk storage, and related industries, and the American Electronics Association (AEA), the 3,000 member grassroots high-technology trade group that spans the industry, asked RAND to undertake a study of this problem, to estimate the resulting magnitude of industry and societal losses, and to provide recommendations on possible strategies for meeting the challenge posed by high-technology hardware theft. Thus, the purpose of this report is to document the results of our study, which addressed four principal questions:

1. What are the total direct losses to high-technology industry that are attributable to theft of high-technology merchandise?

2. In addition to these direct losses, what other costs are being incurred at the firm, industry, and societal level as a result of high-technology hardware theft?

3. To what extent have past security measures succeeded?

4. Given the costs and burden of high-technology hardware theft, what cost-effective policy actions should be considered by firms, industry as a whole, law enforcement organizations, and policy-makers?

Our results rely on an incident-level data collection tool, the Theft Incident Reporting System (TIRS), which was designed to facilitate the standardized reporting of data on incidents and costs of theft. TIRS reports, obtained over a nine-month reporting period from firms representing 40 percent of sales volume in the computer, semiconductor, hard disk drive, and cellular phone industries, laid the foundation for the analyses that projected total direct and indirect losses. Though additional, potential losses were not considered, because of the limited scope of the study and the availability of data, our estimate is that total direct and indirect losses due to theft from manufacturers and distributors sum to over $1 billion annually. In addition, thefts from customers could cost U.S. based manufacturers an additional $4 billion a year. Thus, total direct and indirect losses could exceed $5 billion annually, amounting to roughly 2 percent of industry sales.

This report describes our study methods and explains the components of our total cost estimate. In addition, it documents patterns of theft showing that high-margin firms and their high-margin products are disproportionately victimized because of the added vulnerability of their products. It also discusses the fact that there have been recent reductions in theft rates and reportedly successful collaboration between industry and law enforcement, suggesting that there are high economic returns to security investments and private-public interventions to mitigate theft consequences at the firm, industry, and societal levels.

STUDY METHODS

Several research methods were employed in conducting this study. First, 95 firms with U.S.-based operations were surveyed between September 1997 and June 1998 to collect information on their theft experiences. (Appendix A describes our data collection protocols and TIRS instrument.) These 95 companies represent approximately 40 percent of the sales volume for the four high-tech industries we studied. Next, econometric methodologies were utilized to identify important patterns in the data and provide estimates for the whole high-tech hardware industry, including companies that did not participate in the survey. Simulation models were developed to assess the likely magnitude of indirect costs, including security expenses, the value of lost (or displaced) sales, and the costs of market adjustments made in response to the increased cost of doing business. These models also enabled us to assess costs in terms of who bears them—the victimized company, other firms in the industry, or customers. Finally, in-depth case study interviews were conducted with nine firms and with law enforcement officials. These interviews provided valuable insights on the role and contribution of interventions tried by the firms and law enforcement partners.

SUMMARY OF FINDINGS

Direct Costs of Hardware Theft Are Almost $250 Million

Based on TIRS data provided by surveyed firms, the estimated annual high-tech hardware loss amounts to almost $250 million in direct replacement costs. This loss represents only about one-tenth of 1 percent (0.1 percent) of sales revenue. Most of the lost dollars (almost 80 percent) result from a small number (less than 5 percent) of incidents involving thefts of merchandise worth more than $100,000. Over 70 percent of the reported losses occurred while product was in transit.

The hardware losses of individual firms appear to vary predictably with market conditions. On average, losses are almost directly proportional to the total cost of goods sold. However, losses for high-margin firms (and, by implication, high-margin products) are much higher. When other factors are held constant, high-end products, such as workstations, are also more likely to be stolen. This suggests that new, state-of-the-art products in high demand are particularly vulnerable.

Magnitude of Indirect Losses Exceeds That of Direct Losses by a Factor Greater Than Five

Although the direct losses associated with high-tech hardware theft may seem trivial, on average, they represent only the tip of the iceberg. Indirect costs, which include expensive theft-reduction strategies, lost sales, and other market adjustments, can dwarf direct costs. An illustrative example of a representative firm facing moderate competition and earning average profit margins is presented in Figure S.1. If such a firm experiences hardware losses valued at $1 million, its indirect losses, including increased security investments and lost sales, would total an additional $1.8 million. Also, sales would be displaced from other firms, amounting to another $1.0 million in loss to the industry at large. Finally, customers would suffer losses totaling $2.4 million as firms raise prices in reaction to the higher cost of doing business. For this example, total costs to society are over six times the original hardware cost. For the products that are most likely to be the preferred targets of thieves, these other costs can be even higher. Although precise estimates are not possible, the indirect costs of theft from manufacturers and distributors could total over $1 billion.

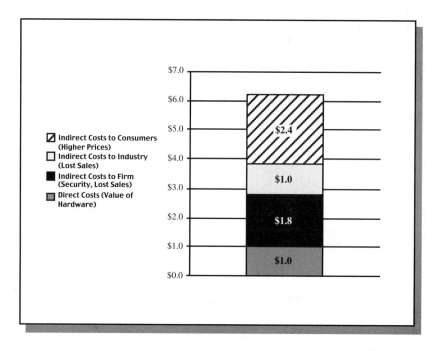

Figure S.1—An Illustrative Example of Indirect Costs of Hardware Theft

Industry Losses Include Cost of Thefts from Business Customers

Products stolen from customers rather than from the high-tech hardware firms themselves can also have a large impact on the bottom line of manufacturers. If customers react to the expected probabilities of theft by reducing their willingness to pay for products, much of the cost will be passed on to manufacturers. On the basis of the incidence of theft from the corporate and administrative offices of our sample firms, we estimate that at least $4 billion of high-tech goods in use may be stolen from U.S. industry as a whole on an annual basis. And this dollar figure may understate the problem, since it includes only U.S. based companies and property stolen from nonbusiness customers.

Total Losses Could Exceed $5 Billion

The sum of the direct and indirect losses exceeds $5 billion, representing about 2 percent of industry revenues and a much higher percentage of net income. And it is essential to note that we have not considered several other, possibly important losses. No data were available on losses from retail outlets or on potentially significant second-order effects—i.e., those associated with business disruptions and loss of valuable data or work product. These effects, which may be particularly pronounced for computers taken from business locations nationwide, could dramatically inflate the measure of economic costs, many of which would be passed on to the high-tech industries.

Industry and Customers Share the Price of High-Tech Losses

When stolen product flows into markets served by victimized firms, the result is large losses because of displaced sales. These losses are only partially borne by the firm actually losing the hardware, however: the smaller the market share of the victimized firm, the more likely that stolen equipment will displace sales of the victimized firm's competitors. Also, in response to the increased costs of doing business (due to security investments and anticipated hardware losses), firms will change the prices at which they sell product and buy components. As a result, their suppliers and customers will bear a portion of the total costs. In many situations likely to prevail in the high-tech industries we studied, these costs of doing business are considerable and can exceed the size of the direct cost by a multiple of two or three depending on the prevailing sales margins and degree of competition.

Firms Don't Have the Correct Incentives to Invest in Security Measures

As illustrated in Figure S.1, the external costs—those borne by the competitors, suppliers, and customers of the victimized firms—can represent a significant portion of the total costs of high-tech hardware theft. Depending on the underlying technological and market circumstances, they can range from 40 to 75 percent of the total cost. This implies that individual firms will not always have appropriate incentives to invest in security measures that could potentially help the industry and society at large. For example, for a company with a small market share, the return on an investment in security may not exceed investment costs at this level. Given that many firms will not have incentives to increase security individually, collective industry actions whereby everyone increases security may be necessary.

There Has Been a Significant Decline in Hardware Theft

Based on data gathered via a supplemental mail survey of a subset of the largest firms participating in TIRS, we found that direct hardware losses have declined dramatically since 1996. This decline was at least 50 percent and may have been as high as 75 percent. Many firms made significant investments in private security measures over this time period, and, although causation is hard to establish, firms that increased their security budgets the most over this period also experienced the greatest declines in stolen hardware. The data are certainly consistent with the conclusion that these security investments had very high returns. However, successful interventions on the part of the public law enforcement community likely played a parallel role. Another potential contributor to recent declines may be changing market conditions, such as increased competition and lower margins in the industries we studied. Significant shifts in supply-and-demand ratios have occurred for some products (e.g., memory chips) in recent years.

POLICY IMPLICATIONS FOR FIRMS, INDUSTRY, AND THE PUBLIC SECTOR

Recent security measures adopted by individual firms appear to have earned very high returns. Even if one ignores the indirect costs and second-order effects, firms appear to earn more than a dollar for each additional dollar they spend on security. Thus, it appears that more investments are warranted. For the future, the largest payoff seems to be associated with being able to better anticipate the vulnerability of products (e.g., new, state-of-the-art, high-margin goods) to theft and with devising targeted prevention measures. Also, there is currently a shortage of (complete) information about the costs and implications of overseas losses, inventory variances, warranty fraud, and counterfeiting. These could be fruitful areas for improved loss reporting, further study, and future intervention.

Our analysis suggests that a large portion of the total costs of hardware theft are not borne by the victimized firm. Rather, much of the cost is passed on to other firms and customers. This suggests a larger role for collective action on the part of the industry and public sector. Current industry initiatives (such as the Technology Asset Protection Association) focusing on standards for shipping freight are good examples. Additional collaboration on serialization and "poison cookies" that help identify and disable stolen property would help address the significant costs stemming from the theft of final product from the offices and facilities of final business customers. Finally, society could well benefit from additional efforts that facilitate information exchanges between industry and law enforcement agencies and increased collaboration in tracking the threat, anticipating the most likely future targets, and combining resources to mount an even more effective campaign against high-tech hardware thieves.

ACKNOWLEDGMENTS

We wish to thank the American Electronics Association (AEA), International Electronics Security Group (IESG) and the following corporate members for their sponsorship of this study: Advanced Micro Devices; Amdahl Corporation; Compaq Computer Corporation, including its Digital Equipment Corporation and Tandem divisions; Consolidated Freightways; Hewlett-Packard Company; IBM Corporation; Intel Corporation; LAM Research; Motorola, Inc.; National Semiconductor; Quantum Corporation; Seagate Technology, Inc.; Sun Microsystems; Technology Theft Prevention Foundation; Texas Instruments, Inc.; Western Digital; and 3COM. In particular, we would like to thank the following members of the oversight committee that provided us with guidance throughout the study: John O'Loughlin, Sun Microsystems; Mike McQuade, American Electronics Association; Pete Costner, Advanced Micro Devices; Devra Dallman, Hewlett-Packard Company; Chris Fedrow, National Semiconductor; and Skip Williams, Texas Instruments.

We also wish to thank Colin Elrod of 3COM and Bill Eyres of The Eyres Group for their valuable assistance, particularly in the early phases of the study. And we want to thank the other members of the IESG for their invaluable assistance and feedback over the course of this study: Tom Pardoe and David Hull, Apple Computer; Ed Rana, Avnet; Grant Crabtree, Compaq Computer Corporation; Tony Gentilucci, Digital Equipment Corporation; Dave Small and Steven Lund, Intel Corporation; Ed Loyd, LAM Research; Rick Pitocco, Motorola, Inc.; Dennis Pardini, Quantum Corporation; Ed Nobis, Seagate Technology, Inc.; and Michael John, Tandem. Finally, although we cannot identify them because of our promise of confidentiality to all participating companies, we wish to acknowledge the assistance of the security directors and the technical and support staff in all of the firms that participated in this study.

We also acknowledge and thank Judith Bailey of the Information Technology Industry Council; Gail Toth of the Transportation Loss Prevention Security Council of the American Trucking Association; Ed Badolato, National Cargo Security Council; the Semiconductor Industry Association; Dave Dasgupta, of the Insurance Services Office; Madine Singer, Insurance Information Institute; Tom Cornwell, of the Technology Theft Prevention Foundation; Rich Bernes, Technology Theft Prevention Foundation; IC Insights of Phoenix, Arizona; Safeware Insurance of Columbus, Ohio; Barry Wilkins, BJSI, Inc.; Patrice Rapalus, Computer Security Institute; and the Bureau of the Census, U.S. Department of Commerce. In the law enforcement community, we wish to thank Sergeant Harvey Smith and Officer Tom Swain of the California Highway Patrol; Lt. Joe Rogoski, New Jersey State Police Cargo Theft Unit; and Lt. Ed Petow, Metro-Dade County Police Tactical Operations Multi-Agency Cargo Anti-Theft Squad (TOMCATS).

At RAND, we wish to thank Bob Anderson and Adele Palmer for their assistance in the early stages of the project; Terry West for his implementation of and technical support for the Theft Incident Reporting System (TIRS); Jan Hanley for her SAS programming support; Patricia Frick, Jo Levy, Regine Webster, Beverly Weidmer, and Deborah Wesley for assistance with data collection and auditing; Lisa Hochman and Terri Perkins for their administrative support, and Cherie Fields for her particularly valuable support to the project. We also are grateful to Steve Garber and Peter Reuter for their reviews.

AEA	American Electronics Association
ASP	Average Sales Price
CHP	California Highway Patrol
CTIP	Cargo Theft Interdiction Program
FBI	Federal Bureau of Investigation
IESG	International Electronics Security Group
ISO	Insurance Services Organization
ITI	Information Technology Industry Council
NEDA	National Electronics Distributors Association
PC	Personal Computer
PCS	Personal Communication System
TAPA	Technology Asset Protection Association
TIRS	Theft Incident Reporting System
TTPF	Technology Theft Prevention Foundation
UCR	Uniform Crime Report

Chapter One

INTRODUCTION

BACKGROUND

The computer, semiconductor, hard disk drive, and cellular telephone industries are among the key industries in the high-technology sector of the U.S. economy. The demand for products from these industries has grown remarkably over the last decade,[1] arguably providing one of the principal sources of fuel for the U.S. macroeconomic engine:[2]

- Between 1990 and 1997, the value of U.S. shipments of computers and related equipment worldwide is estimated to have increased from $154.8 to $235.5 billion, and U.S. consumption of computers is estimated to have increased from $50.4 to $94.9 billion.[3]

- The U.S. computer equipment industry, furthermore, is estimated to be responsible for nearly three-fourths of the worldwide computer market through its global operations.[4] In 1997

---

[1]One widely cited estimate is that the computer and semiconductor industries have grown at an average annual rate of 17 percent per year.

[2]The American Electronics Association (1997) recently estimated that U.S. high-tech industry accounts for 6.2 percent of gross domestic product (GDP), 4.3 million jobs, including 1.9 million manufacturing jobs, and over $150 billion in exports, making it a main driver of U.S. economic growth.

[3]ITI, 1998, pp. 63, 66.

[4]Benner, 1997.

1

alone, the U.S. is estimated to have exported $22.6 billion in computers and related equipment, and $18.2 billion in parts.

- During the same period, U.S. market consumption of hard disk drives grew from an estimated $14.1 to $17.0 billion.[5]

- The worldwide market in semiconductors grew from an estimated $50.5 billion in 1990 to more than $137.2 billion in 1997.[6]

- Between 1988 and 1995, the estimated number of cellular subscribers increased by over 1500 percent, from 2.1 million to about 33.8 million.

The growing demand for these and related high-tech products has provided a host of attractive new targets of opportunity for criminals. The industries we studied produce high-tech hardware products—computers, semiconductors, hard disk drives, cellular phones, and other components—that are valuable, compact, and easy to transport. For example, a suitcase of microprocessors is worth more than an equivalent volume of cocaine, is more difficult to trace than cash, and is not a felony to have in one's possession. The criminal activity associated with these high-tech items, which involves dishonest employees, organized crime, urban gangs, and quasi-legitimate distributors, is believed by some industry observers to total billions of dollars.[7] Not surprisingly, the companies that manufacture and distribute these products probably bear the greatest losses. We thus focused our analysis on these manufacturing and distributing firms.[8]

Decisionmakers in industry and the government are grappling with the implications of this form of high-tech crime and have lacked key information on the scope and magnitude of the problem. Estimates of industry-wide losses are largely based on anecdote rather than data, and systematic attempts to gather data on the scale and nature of the problem to date have failed.

---

[5]Benner, p. 69.

[6]Semiconductor Industry Association, World Semiconductor Trade Statistics, global billings report history.

[7]For example, see Goodfriend and Wilkins, 1996.

[8]Although theft of these products is likely to plague retailers as well, we were unable to obtain data on such incidents.

The International Electronics Security Group (IESG), a consortium of high-technology electronics industry security executives from the computer, semiconductor, hard disk storage, and related industries, and the American Electronics Association (AEA) asked RAND to undertake a study of this problem, to estimate the resulting magnitude of industry and societal losses, and to provide recommendations on possible strategies for meeting the challenge posed by high-tech product theft. Thus, the purpose of this report is to document the results of our study, which addressed four principal questions:

1. What are the total direct losses to high-technology industry that are attributable to theft of high-technology merchandise?

2. In addition to these direct losses, what other costs are being incurred at the firm, industry, and societal level as a result of high-technology hardware theft?

3. To what extent have past security measures succeeded?

4. Given the costs and burden of high-technology hardware theft, what cost-effective policy actions should be considered by firms, industry as a whole, law enforcement organizations, and policymakers?

THE MANY DIMENSIONS OF HIGH-TECH HARDWARE THEFT

Many aspects of high-tech hardware theft were considered in our investigation. We considered different types of incidents, such as thefts from warehouses and manufacturing facilities. Some of these thefts were armed robberies; others can be characterized as "disappearing" inventory. We also considered incidents that took place while product was in transit, including violent truck hijackings and packages that failed to reach the final destination for unknown reasons. We also gathered and evaluated data describing thefts from corporate offices. In this case we focused primarily on thefts from the offices of hardware producers and distributors, although we believe that these experiences also shed light on thefts from the offices of other business customers. We did not consider thefts from non-business or residential customers or from retail outlets.[9]

Hardware thefts create multiple levels of costs, all of which we considered. In addition to the direct costs of replacing stolen equipment, there are other, indirect market effects. Of these, we evaluated the increased costs of security, lost/displaced sales (i.e., those that are lost when potential customers purchase gray or black market goods), and the economic consequences of market adjustments such as the price increases that inevitably occur. We also considered a number of second-order effects even though we were unable to provide quantitative estimates of their importance. These include disruptions in business, delayed shipments, and production stoppages. Other second-order effects include the cost of servicing invalid warranties on stolen equipment that may have been damaged or installed improperly.

The important question of who bears the cost of high-tech product theft was also investigated. Although victimized firms bear the cost of replacing stolen equipment and have to pay for their own investments in security, they normally adjust their prices to pass on a portion of this burden to suppliers and final customers. In addition, while the targeted firm may experience displaced sales because of theft, so too may that firm's competitors: the person who purchases a new computer advertised in the local newspaper at a bargain price may have otherwise purchased a competitor's brand through normal channels.

METHOD

Our approach to the problem entailed

- Conducting an initial round of interviews with firms in different high-tech hardware industries to clarify the range and scope of questions and issues that needed to be addressed or considered, and to identify potential sources of data.

---

[9]Efforts to recruit participation of several retail outlets were not successful.

- Collecting revenue and market data on principal U.S. high-tech industries—computers, hard disk drives, semiconductors (particularly microprocessors and computer memories), cellular telephones/personal communication systems (PCS), and distributors of these products.

- Designing and fielding a Web-based survey instrument—the Theft Incident Reporting System (TIRS)—to a sampling of firms that represented approximately 40 percent of U.S. high-tech industry sales revenue. (Appendix A describes our data collection instrument, sample, and protocols.)

- Collecting nine months' worth of data (October 1997 through June 1998) on individual firms' high-tech theft experiences using TIRS.

- Collecting relevant revenue and other financial data, as well as market size, share, and other industry data for reporting firms.

- Conducting a series of in-depth case studies with nine representative firms.

- Interviewing representatives from selected law enforcement agencies.

- Conducting quarterly audits of TIRS data.

- Fielding a final mail questionnaire to participating firms to collect data that would sharpen our ability to interpret the TIRS data properly.

- Using statistical models to identify systematic patterns in the reported losses and to generate a reliable estimate of total industrywide high-tech theft losses.

- Using economic market simulation models to assess the indirect costs to firms, industry, and society as a whole.

ORGANIZATION OF THIS REPORT

Chapter Two provides our estimate of annual total direct losses attributable to high-tech hardware theft from manufacturers and distributors of computers, semiconductors, hard disk drives, and cellular telephones. It also reports the results of statistical analyses designed to describe systematic patterns in the loss experiences of firms. Chapter Three turns to the question of the indirect costs of theft, including security investments, lost sales, and market adjustments. We also consider the importance of losses from business customers of high-tech manufacturers. This chapter concludes with a discussion of the more significant second-order effects identified by participating firms. In Chapter Four, we consider recent declines in the magnitude of hardware thefts and assess the probable role of security investments in causing the observed trends. We conclude, in Chapter Five, with a discussion of policy implications from the perspective of individual firms, industry as a whole, and the public sector.

Chapter Two

THE DIRECT COSTS OF HIGH-TECH HARDWARE THEFT

This chapter presents our findings regarding the direct costs to firms of replacing high-technology hardware stolen from manufacturers and distributors. The chapter begins with a description of our estimate of direct losses, follows that with a description of key patterns in the loss data, and then analyzes factors that can predict the level of losses experienced by individual firms.

ESTIMATE OF INDUSTRY DIRECT LOSSES

Between October 1997 and June 1998, our sample of 95 participating firms reported a total of 1,704 theft incidents for a total direct loss value of $34.7 million. To obtain an estimate of annual industry losses, we made several adjustments to the sample data:

- corrections for underreported or missing information,

- projections for nonparticipating firms, and

- extrapolation for a complete calendar year.

On numerous occasions, participating firms reported that incident data were incomplete. In some cases, firms admitted that certain classes of thefts, such as low-value incidents and international losses, were not recorded by security. In such cases, we filled in missing data based on the firms' reported estimates of the shortfalls. On average, firms estimated that 44 percent of total losses were not reported through TIRS. In other cases, merchandise losses (number of

7

units, type of equipment) were reported, but no dollar value for the replacement cost (production or wholesale price) was given. We multiplied the number of units reported stolen by the average per-unit value reported by other firms to gain an estimate of the dollar loss.

As indicated earlier, the 95 participating firms had total sales representing approximately 40 percent of aggregate revenues for the computer, semiconductor, hard drive, and cell telephone industries. Sample losses, adjusted for the missing and incomplete data deficiencies described above, were scaled up by industry, under the assumption that nonparticipating firms had the same theft experience (per unit of sales) as those contributing actual loss data.[1]

Finally, since data were collected for only nine months, we multiplied all numbers by 4/3 to obtain annual estimates. Since we observed no seasonal patterns (holding sales constant) over the fourth quarter of 1997 and the first two quarters of 1998, we assumed that the third quarter was similar to the other three in terms of theft rates.

The above calculations led to an annual loss estimate for the replacement cost of stolen hardware of $247 million.[2] This represents only about 0.1 percent (one-tenth of 1 percent) of total industry revenues. Since some of these losses are multiplicative, this figure understates the economic significance of direct hardware losses. For example, semiconductors and hard drives are components of the final computer products. To the extent that component theft affects

---

[1]We have no reason to believe that the sample of participating firms is unrepresentative of the larger industry. For example, IBM was one of the largest nonparticipants. Based on our extrapolation methodology, we project that IBM suffered between $20 and $30 million in direct losses during the 12 month period ending in September 1998. According to public statements by IBM representatives, actual losses for 1997 fell within that range.

[2]Participating firms reported $34.7 million in losses. On average, firms reported that this represented about 56 percent of their actual experience. These firms represented 37 percent of the relevant industry segment. To illustrate, 34.7/(.56 x .37) times 1.33 = $223 million. We did this calculation for each quarter, using individual firm estimates of underreporting to obtain the $247 million figure. Although comparable data on all losses do not exist, our data for in-transit thefts in California can be compared with information provided by the California Highway Patrol, "Cargo Theft Summary Data for the Period," August 1998. The CHP data indicate $18 million in cargo thefts during the 12 month period ending in September 1998. Using TIRS data, we estimate the loss to be $23 million based on reported hijackings in California.

costs (and therefore prices) in the final computer market, these losses need to be compounded (along with wholesale and retail theft rates) to assess the overall economic impact. However, even tripling the small fraction represents a small fraction of the affected sectors.

KEY PATTERNS IN THE LOSS DATA

Armed with company-level data losses, we were able to perform a more detailed analysis of the high-tech industry's theft experience. We present here information on the patterns of losses among firms reporting their losses to TIRS, categorizing the losses by, for example, value per incident, product type, theft incident scenario, and theft location in the firm's manufacturing cycle.

Losses by Value

One view frequently encountered in press reporting on high-tech hardware theft is that the value of the average theft is quite high, often characterized as being in the hundreds of thousands of dollars.[3] The TIRS data reflect a somewhat different picture.

The total losses reported to TIRS amounted to $34.7 million from 1,704 incidents, for an average (mean) value of about $20,000 per incident. Looking at the frequency with which the various losses occurred, however, suggests a much lower value for the median incident.

Figure 2.1 presents data on the percentages of theft incidents and losses by loss value. As can be seen, the most common thefts (accounting for 80 percent of the theft incidents but only 6 percent of the total losses) are those with a loss value of less than $5,000, which means that the typical (median) theft is only about $2,000.[4] However, the figure also shows that it is the high-value incidents that ac-

---

[3]The FBI has estimated the average cost of a high-tech crime at $450,000. Mello (1997) reported that, according to the Technology Theft Prevention Foundation, a nonprofit group founded by insurance giant Chubb, of Warren, New Jersey, the average loss from a computer hardware theft is $750,000.

[4]The median is the value at the 50th percentile of the distribution, which means an equal number of cases were higher and lower than this value.

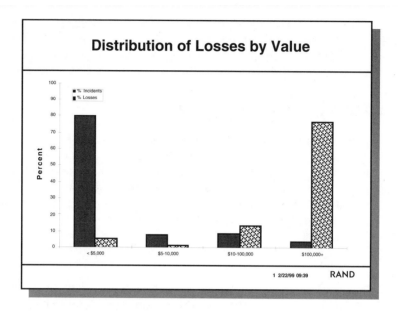

Figure 2.1—Distribution of Incidents and Losses by Value

count for the majority share of total losses: while only 4 percent of the incidents involved losses of $100,000 or more, this 4 percent accounted for over 60 percent of total company losses. Thus, while the average high-tech hardware theft is probably in the low thousands of dollars, it is the high-value thefts that dominate overall company losses.[5] The implication of this finding is that firms should focus on finding ways to reduce these low-probability but high-value thefts.

Losses by Product Category

We also sought to understand how losses were distributed among the various intermediate and final products that flow through the high-tech industry. As shown in Table 2.1, the four types of products that

---

[5]As will be seen below, cargo thefts of high-tech products typically involve larger losses than do cargo thefts of non-high-technology products.

were the principal focus of this study—computers, semiconductors, hard disk drives, and cellular telephones—accounted for almost 90 percent of the hardware losses that were reported in TIRS.[6]

As the table shows,

- Semiconductors were the target of thefts in 10.7 percent of the incidents but accounted for 24.0 percent of the value. Most of

Table 2.1

Incidents and Losses by Product Category

Product Category	% Incidents	% Losses
Semiconductors (all types)	10.7	24.0
of which:		
Microprocessors	6.3	12.8
Computer memory	4.0	8.6
Other semiconductors	0.4	2.6
Handheld cellular/PCS/pagers	4.2	21.3
Computers (all types)	44.0	26.8
of which:		
Microcomputers/PCs	3.8	8.3
Laptop/notebook/palmtop PCs	31.8	9.0
Desktop workstations	7.2	5.3
Network file servers	0.6	4.0
Other computers	0.6	0.2
Hard disk drives	32.9	16.0
Other final products	8.2	11.9

SOURCE: Theft Incident Reporting System.

---

[6]See Appendix A for the complete merchandise code list of product categories.

the semiconductor losses were attributable to microprocessors (12.8 percent) and computer memory (8.6 percent); other semiconductors accounted for only 2.6 percent.

- Handheld cellular telephones, PCS, and pagers were involved in only 4.2 percent of the incidents but accounted for a total of 21.3 percent of the losses.

- Computers of all kinds were targeted in about 44 percent of the incidents and accounted for 26.8 percent of the losses, with portable computers being the most frequently targeted type of computer.

- Hard disk drives were targeted in 32.9 percent of the incidents and accounted for 16.0 percent of the losses.

- Other final products, such as printers and other peripheral hardware, represented 11.9 percent of lost value.

Taken together, these findings suggest that computers (primarily portable computers) and hard disk drives are the most frequently targeted high-tech hardware, but that semiconductors and cellular telephones and other personal communication devices are accounting for the largest value share of losses among TIRS-participating companies.

Thefts by Incident Scenario

Another view of high-tech hardware theft is provided by looking at theft incidents by type of crime. Table 2.2 breaks reported losses out by incident scenario.

As shown in the table, most of the reported theft incidents were simple property crimes of various types—simple theft, burglary, and inventory shrinkage. These accounted for 60.7 percent of the total incidents and 56.1 percent of the losses whose theft scenarios were reported. Thus, these should be viewed as lower-bound estimates. However, for many of the incidents, no scenario was reported.

While armed robbery and hijacking were rare, they accounted for total losses that were out of proportion to their share of incidents.

Table 2.2

Incidents and Losses by Incident Scenario

Scenario Type	% Incidents	% Losses
Theft (without break-in or force)	55.7	45.4
Burglary	4.1	10.2
Attempted burglary	0.2	—
Shrinkage/inventory loss	0.7	0.5
Armed robbery	0.2	3.0
Attempted armed robbery	0.1	—
Hijacking	1.5	17.9

SOURCE: Theft Incident Reporting System.
NOTE: Percentages do not add to 100 due to missing data.

For example, there were only four armed robberies (about 0.2 percent of the total incidents), but they yielded for the perpetrators a total of $1 million, or about 3 percent of the total reported losses. Hijackings, which accounted for about 1.5 percent of the total incidents, also accounted for 17.9 percent of the total theft losses.

Geographic Patterns

We now turn to the geographic patterning in theft losses. The data reported to TIRS suggest that three-quarters of the incidents and about half of the hardware losses occurred in the United States (see Table 2.3).

The data in the table suggest that

- The United States and Europe are the regions accounting for the greatest share of theft incidents and losses, in part at least because they are the largest consumers of high-tech products.

- By comparison, other parts of the western hemisphere (Canada and Latin America) and Asia account for a much smaller share of the reported losses, only a little over 7 percent.

- The "other" category, we believe, may be due to the vagaries of locating where losses occur when product is being shipped between continents.

Table 2.3

Incidents and Losses by Geographic Region

Region	% Incidents	% Losses
United States	73.3	50.4
Europe	7.4	30.7
Other western hemisphere	1.7	4.1
Asia	2.9	3.0
Other	7.9	7.6
Unknown	4.5	4.0

SOURCE: Theft Incident Reporting System.

However, the proportions accounted for by non-U.S. losses could in fact be somewhat larger than shown, because the probability that small losses will be underreported appears to be higher for foreign than for U.S. locations. For some companies, underreporting stems from the fact that foreign operations enjoy a fair degree of autonomy from corporate headquarters and thus are not required to report all losses to corporate security managers. For other companies, incident reporting systems in the U.S. facilities are not in place in overseas operations. As a result, we expect that the information on foreign losses is less reliable and that such losses might constitute an even larger percentage than is suggested by the raw TIRS data.[7]

Location of Thefts

We also collected data enabling us to understand where thefts were occurring in firms' production and distribution processes. As shown in Table 2.4, "in transit" was the most commonly reported theft location in the manufacturing and distribution process, accounting for fully 59.5 percent of the total reported losses. If one ignores incidents for which the theft scenario is unknown, this figure rises to about 71.6 percent.

---

[7]For a report suggesting that thieves are more active abroad because of U.S. law enforcement's effectiveness, see "High Tech Thieves Head to Greener Pasture: Europe," *EETimes*, May 22, 1996.

Table 2.4

Incidents and Losses by Location in Manufacturing Cycle

Location	% Incidents	% Unadj. Losses
In transit	42.6	58.8
Corporate/administration area	26.1	8.6
Company manufacture/assembly area	7.8	4.8
Company warehouse/inventory	2.0	4.5
Company loading, distribution, traffic	1.3	1.5
Company other property	2.0	0.4
Subcontractor facility	0.2	0.5
Unreported/missing	18.0	20.9

SOURCE: Theft Incident Reporting System.

PREDICTING COMPANY LOSS EXPERIENCES

We conducted an econometric analysis of the quarterly losses reported by participating firms to look for systematic patterns in the data. (See Appendix C, where the results are summarized in Table C.1.) The estimated model linked aggregate losses by firm by quarter with a set of potential predictors, including the cost of goods sold, the firms' net profit margins, and variables measuring the percentages of firm revenue attributed to sales of workstations, hard drives, cellular phones, and semiconductors.

The results of the analysis indicate that expected losses expand nearly in direct proportion to the total volume of wholesale value, all things held equal. For example, a 100 percent increase in the cost of goods leads to a 94 percent increase in losses. High-margin firms (and products) are also more vulnerable. The estimates indicate that for a firm earning margins 20 percentage points higher than those of another firm (as in the case of manufacturers of microprocessors versus manufacturers of hard disk drives), expected losses would normally be 76 percent. Thus, since new, state-of-the-art products can have margins that are even higher, the loss experience could be three or four times higher for products that are in the greatest demand.

The estimates also indicate that high-end equipment is especially vulnerable. Workstation producers suffer losses triple those of low-end PC producers (holding other factors constant), and hard drive producers also suffer higher losses. In contrast, cellular phone and semiconductor producers have lower theft rates. Other models that included quarterly indicator variables indicate that seasonal effects are not pronounced when seasonal variation in revenues is controlled for. Most systematic variations are due to typical fluctuations in sales and net income, which have a seasonal pattern.

Chapter Three

THE INDIRECT COSTS OF HIGH-TECH
HARDWARE THEFT

The total cost of replacing hardware stolen from high-technology manufacturers and distributors was estimated to be almost $250 million annually. However, this tabulation ignores the additional costs that are borne by the victimized firm and its competitors, suppliers, and customers. These indirect costs can be placed in the following categories:

- displaced demand (lost sales) that occurs when potential customers acquire stolen equipment through the gray or black market,

- security investments by firms to avoid and investigate theft and insurance,

- costs stemming from pricing increases as firms act to pass higher costs on to customers,

- market consequences borne by manufacturers when final products are stolen from their customers, and

- second-order, or side, effects that occur when goods are stolen.

For the first four categories—displaced demand, security investments, pricing adjustments, and market consequences—we assessed their importance using simulation models. We concluded that these indirect costs are substantial. For the last category—second-order effects—no data were readily available for evaluating the magnitude of the associated costs. We thus evaluated their possible importance on the basis of our interviews and available survey data.

DISPLACED DEMAND, OR LOST SALES

In addition to incurring cost increases, firms can expect to lose sales as a result of hardware theft. Stolen goods end up in the hands of firms or private individuals that might otherwise have been willing to purchase the product through normal channels. The degree to which this is true depends on the particular product, the demand for that product, and the market that ends up receiving stolen property.[1] Although stolen items may not be viewed as perfect substitutes for product sold through legitimate channels, some significant degree of displacement is probable. Security officials reported that much stolen product ends up being resold via traditional distribution channels or by retail outlets that compete with those acquiring products directly from manufacturers.

When demand displacement occurs, firms lose more than just the cost of replacing the stolen items. They also lose the opportunity to earn profits on the sale of the product. When net margins are high, as they often are for the favored targets of opportunity for thieves, this loss can be considerable.

It is important to note that lost sales may be suffered not only by the firm directly victimized. When firms sell products that are viewed as substitutes for each other, all firms can lose sales when stolen product becomes available to some market segment. For example, a low-priced computer made available through the gray market might well draw business away from other computer manufacturers. The degree to which lost sales are suffered by the victimized firm as opposed to the rest of the industry segment depends, in large part, on the degree to which products are similar and whether relevant markets are highly concentrated. For a dominant firm in the microprocessor industry, a hardware loss will primarily displace sales of that firm. For firms in more competitive industries, such as those that produce disk drives or computers, demand displacement will be spread across many competitors. The result in this latter case is that a large portion of the indirect costs of theft from a particular firm are borne by other firms in the industry.

---

[1] The roles of product demand and the nature of end markets are explored in Appendix B.

SECURITY INVESTMENTS AND INSURANCE

The threat of high-tech hardware theft induces firms to invest in security measures designed to reduce losses. Company initiatives that we observed include the hardening of facilities via capital improvements and the hiring of armed escorts. Some firms have changed their human resources practices, using more stringent processes for personnel screening and background investigations. Other companies have become more active in the quality assurance of freight forwarders and in negotiating more-secure methods for shipping product. Many of the largest firms regularly conduct their own investigations in support of the efforts of local, state, and federal law enforcement officials. Based on our survey of firms participating in TIRS, security expenditures directly attributable to the reduction of high-tech hardware theft currently total approximately $300 million per year, less than one-third of total losses.[2]

Firms have changed their business operations in a variety of other ways in response to high-tech hardware theft. For example, many firms use more-discreet packaging so that valuable contents are not readily identifiable by thieves. Other companies have instituted more-careful controls to reduce shrinkage. Although such changes are not reflected as line items in security budgets, they clearly increase the expense of conducting business and should be part of the overall accounting of the costs of hardware theft. Some of these security costs can be viewed as fixed investments (such as the hardening of capital assets), while others (such as the use of inventory controls) increase the marginal or per-unit cost of doing business.

In our final mail questionnaire (see Appendix A), we asked firms about their insurance coverage for losses due to hardware theft. We found that many firms were self-insured. Many others had high deductibles or liability limits. Even in cases where there was applicable insurance, premiums were adjusted annually based on theft experience. On average, firms received reimbursements summing to only 25 percent of the lost value in merchandise. Of course, there is no reimbursement for indirect costs.

---

[2]In Chapter Four, we present additional detail about the kinds of security measures firms have adopted and offer some evidence concerning the return on these investments.

PRICING INCREASES DUE TO INCREASED COSTS

Firms that are potential victims of hardware theft face higher costs of producing and distributing their products. This is because a certain percentage of output will be lost to thieves, and because security measures and other operational changes in response to increased threats increase the marginal cost of production for each unit of product that makes it to the final market. In such circumstances, firms confront the same incentives facing any business that endures a cost increase. That is, depending on market conditions, they pass some of the cost on to consumers in the form of price increases. In addition, they adjust their demand for inputs to reflect the higher cost of doing business. For example, higher costs incurred by a computer manufacturer will partially end up as a *higher* price for computers and also as a *lower* price for computer components, such as microprocessors. In other words, a portion, but not all, of the hardware loss is borne by suppliers and customers. In fact, it does not matter where along the chain of production, distribution, and re-tail sales the actual theft occurs. Nor does it matter which firm is li-able for the immediate loss. Given time, prices adjust so that all market participants incur some share of the costs.

EFFECTS ON MANUFACTURERS OF THEFTS FROM FINAL BUSINESS CUSTOMERS

The previous discussion suggests that hardware thefts from cus-tomers have the same impact as thefts directly from the manufac-turer. This proposition is formally demonstrated in Appendix B.[3] The intuition is as follows. Thefts from business customers implicitly increase the price of using targeted hardware. If businesses have ex-pectations that they will lose a certain percentage of equipment through theft, they will anticipate a higher cost, on average, of using the same level of capital services in the future. In fact, the implied price will increase by the same percentage as the expected theft rate. This price rise will cause a decrease in demand for the product. Even though customers will usually replace stolen property, the expecta-

---

[3]This general result is well known in economics, particularly the literature on public finance. For example, the incidence (who bears the cost?) of a value-added tax on pro-ducers, a sales tax on retailers, and a consumption tax on consumers is identical.

tion of higher costs due to theft will force manufacturers to lower retail prices overall. The resulting decline in manufacturers' profit is
similar (if not identical) to the decline caused by direct theft. In addition, to the extent that stolen equipment, especially new hardware
that has yet to be installed, displaces product that would have been
sold directly to other potential customers through legitimate markets, manufacturers and their suppliers suffer still greater losses.

Although we made no effort to survey a wide range of business or
individual customers, our survey of high-tech manufacturers provides important insights into the magnitude of this problem. We
noted, in Chapter Two, that about 9 percent of reported hardware
losses, representing over $20 million in direct costs, involved thefts
from corporate offices. Recall that this equipment is part of the
installed base (or soon to be installed base) of high-tech hardware
currently in use. There is no reason to believe that other business
customers do not incur theft rates of the same order of magnitude.[4]

The high-tech industries sampled represent about 0.5 percent (one-
half of 1 percent) of white-collar employment in the U.S. economy. If
other industries are experiencing equivalent theft rates, business
customers could be losing as much as $4 billion in hardware, evalu-
ated at retail prices ($20 million divided by 0.005). This number is
most likely an *understatement* of actual losses, because it ignores
losses from foreign business and residential customers and does not
account for the likely underreporting of losses for this category of
theft, particularly for the international locations of domestic manufacturers. Although precise quantification is not possible, it would
not be unreasonable to conclude that $4 billion in thefts from final
consumers will end up costing producers an equivalent amount.

SIMULATING THE EFFECTS OF INDIRECT COSTS

Although data on the dollar amounts of the aforementioned market
adjustments are not available, it is possible to simulate the range of
likely effects using spreadsheet models based on representations of

---

[4]It is possible, though not obvious, that high-tech manufacturers utilize more computers than other industries. This would tend to overstate the theft incidence nationwide. However, this potential bias is probably more than offset by other factors
mentioned below.

the microeconomics of relevant high-tech markets. The details of the model specifications and a set of illustrative simulations are presented in Appendix B. Briefly, the models assume the following:

- firms seek to maximize profits,

- market price is a function of quantities sold by the firm and its competitors,

- stolen property displaces sales of the victimized firm and its competitors to varying degrees,

- security measures increase either fixed or marginal costs of production,

- increases in security reduce the theft rate, but there are diminishing marginal returns to these investments,

- if security investments are held constant, thefts vary in proportion to the quantity of output,

- firms behave noncooperatively with respect to both security investments and output sold, and

- all competitors face the same threat and can employ the same security measures.

Several model parameters reflecting different market conditions were allowed to vary so that we could assess the resulting impact on direct costs. These parameters were

- the number of competitors in the relevant market,

- the degree to which theft displaces sales,

- the extent to which security increases increase marginal or fixed costs, and

- the marginal cost of replacing stolen property.

Table 3.1 provides illustrative results for a range of market circumstances. Our goal was to explore the relative importance of direct

Table 3.1

The Total Costs of Theft: Illustrative Model Simulations for Varying Firm Profiles

	A	B	C	D	E	F
	Direct Theft (replacement)	Firm Losses	Industry Sales Losses	Consumer Losses	Total Losses	Percent External to Firm
					(B+C+D)	(C+D/E)
1. Medium margin, competitive firm						
No lost sales	1.0	0.8	0.0	1.4	2.2	65
High lost sales	1.0	1.0	0.7	2.0	3.7	72
2. High margin, dominant firm						
No lost sales	1.0	1.4	0.0	1.3	2.7	48
High lost sales	1.0	4.7	1.5	2.8	8.8	48
3. Low margin, competitive firm						
No lost sales	1.0	0.9	0.0	1.4	2.3	62
High lost sales	1.0	0.9	0.3	1.7	2.9	69

NOTES: Columns A–E are in millions of dollars.

Column A represents $1 million in direct hardware losses.

Column B represents the total loss suffered by the firm due to the $1 million in direct losses. In addition to direct losses, this column includes security investments and lost sales, but can be partially offset by price increases to customers.

Column C represents lost sales of competitors.

Column D represents losses to customers due to price increases.

Column E represents the sum of losses to the targeted firm, the industry, and consumers.

Column F represents the portion of the total loss that falls to the industry and consumers.

and indirect costs. In all scenarios presented, security investments are assumed to have both a fixed and a marginal cost component.[5] For each market situation analyzed, we compare the two extreme assumptions with respect to demand displacement, i.e., the case in which either 100 percent or none of the stolen hardware results in

---

[5]In Appendix B, we analyze the case where security costs are primarily fixed in nature. In such cases, firms are unlikely to increase prices by as much, at least in the short run. Thus, consumers bear a smaller portion of the increased burden. In addition, we pursue alternative characterizations of the activity of thieves.

lost sales. Intermediate assumptions result in outcomes that fall between the reported outcomes. The reported ratios provide the relative magnitude of economic costs that result from each $1 million of direct theft losses.

For example, the first situation illustrated in Table 3.1 reflects an "average" high-tech firm that faces moderate competition (four equally positioned rivals that split the market). Price-cost margins are modest at 30 percent. Such a situation might reflect circumstances prevailing in the cell phone or computer industry. Column A provides direct losses, indexed to be $1 million. For such a firm, total losses are given by the decline in profits that occurs as a result of this level of theft experience. This outcome includes increased security costs and lost sales and is partially offset by any price increases that the firm has made to recover the higher marginal costs of doing business (because of theft and security costs). When there are no lost sales, an unlikely extreme, the total decline in the firm's profit is actually only $800,000. This reflects some ability on the part of the firm to pass a portion of the increased costs on to consumers.

Note that in the case of high lost sales, external industry losses are $0.7 million, or $700,000. This is because a portion of the lost sales is borne by competitors rather than by the victimized firm. In a competitive industry, where rival firms control a large portion of the market, a smaller percentage of the lost sales is borne by rivals. It is important to note that the effects of displaced sales flow in multiple directions. At the same time that the firm highlighted in our example experiences thefts that reduce sales for its competitors, stolen products from these same competitors have the same effect on the original firm.[6] In addition to the firm and the industry bearing costs, consumers will suffer an economic loss due to price increases. In the case of no lost sales, this loss is $1.4 million. In the case of full displacement, the cost is $2 million. This economic cost to consumers is above and beyond the firm and industry losses. With full demand

---

[6]The simulation model assumes that all five firms in the industry are identical. Thus, at the same time that the $1 million in hardware theft displaces $0.7 million in industry profits, the four rivals, through identical theft losses, could be expected to create the same degree of lost sales for our sample firm. As a result, $0.7 million of the firm's losses could be attributed to the hardware thefts from each rival, not its own hardware losses.

displacement, the original hardware loss of $1 million actually costs society $3.7 million, including $1.0 in firm losses, $0.7 in losses for competitors, and $2.0 million in losses for consumers.[7] The $700,000 in losses stemming from displaced sales from competitors and the $2 million lost by consumers are external costs that represent 72 percent of total losses.

The second set of simulations shown in Table 3.1 is for a dominant firm (with half of the industry sales in its relevant market) selling products with high net margins exceeding 66 percent. This scenario typifies industry segments such as high-end microprocessors. With high margins, firms suffer much larger indirect losses, primarily because the value of lost business (because of higher pricing or displaced sales) is so much greater in comparison with replacement costs. In the case of full demand displacement, costs borne by the firm total $4.7 million. The $1 million in hardware losses directly suffered by the dominant firm cause an even higher burden ($1.5 million) to be imposed on the rest of the industry (in this case, representing 50 percent of the market) due to displaced sales that have a high margin.

In this situation, consumer welfare also diminishes, by $2.8 million, bringing the total losses for a $1 million theft up to nearly $9 million. About half of these losses are borne by consumers and other firms in the industry. Because so much of the social loss is external in these circumstances, the individual firms involved are unlikely to have the incentive needed to take the socially appropriate action of investing in their own security in order to reduce theft rates.

The third scenario in Table 3.1 represents low-margin firms in competitive industries. This circumstance reflects products such as disk drives, which are now viewed as commodities. In such situations, total firm losses are not likely to be much higher than the direct hardware losses. Even in the case of full demand displacement, firm losses (excluding those created by rival firm losses) are about the same as direct hardware losses. However, consumer losses due to price adjustments remain quite high, bringing the total societal loss to between two and three times the original hardware loss.

---

[7] Since this $700,000 in lost sales is due to thefts from rivals, it should be excluded from the accounting of costs stemming from hardware thefts directly from the sample firm.

We have seen that thieves are much more likely to target firms with high margins. This implies that the high-margin scenario is more likely to prevail in the mix of products actually stolen. Thus, it is reasonable to conclude that, industrywide, the magnitude of indirect losses in comparison to that of direct hardware losses would be higher.

SECOND-ORDER EFFECTS OF HARDWARE THEFT

In addition to the direct and indirect costs we have described, there are numerous other, second-order effects that could be quite costly. Although we were unable to measure the magnitude or prevalence of these losses, we surveyed and interviewed a number of firms about the importance of such effects. The following are the areas of greatest concern:

- *Production line stoppages.* Although few of the TIRS-reported incidents involved a line stoppage, many risk managers expressed the belief that this was one of the most feared outcomes resulting from theft. Line stoppages greatly impact not only firm operations, but customer relations as well.

- *Disruption of business operations.* About 10 percent of reporting firms indicated that business operations had been disrupted at least once as a result of thefts. While such disruptions range from minimal to devastating depending on the nature of the operation affected, this is another area of significant concern.

- *Loss of proprietary data.* Approximately three in ten of the responding firms said that valuable data had been lost as a result of thefts on one or more occasions. These losses are likely to be much more significant in the case of computers stolen from corporate offices, including those outside the surveyed high-tech industries.

- *Delays in delivery to customers.* About one in five responding firms reported that high-tech hardware thefts had resulted in at least one delivery delay. Firms were concerned that these delays would significantly harm business customers and violate the terms of their contractual relationships.

- *Threats and injuries to employees.* For a little over 12 percent of responding firms, employees had been injured or threatened during theft incidents occurring during the reporting period.

Now, in Chapter Four, we turn to a discussion of responses firms have made to these threats.

RETURNS ON SECURITY INVESTMENTS

The indirect costs of hardware theft may far exceed the replacement cost of stolen goods. Perhaps more important, many of these indirect costs are not borne by the victimized firm, but rather by suppliers, competitors, and final consumers. Thus, from a social welfare perspective, firms may not have appropriate incentives to invest in security measures. However, firms have increased their security budgets in recent years. According to data we collected, security budgets for firms in high-technology hardware industries rose significantly between 1996 and 1997. When we scale our numbers to the industry level, we estimate that high-tech hardware firms are now spending approximately $300 million annually on security for theft reduction. According to firms we surveyed, this represents about 20 percent of total budgets allocated for security. This chapter describes the measures that participating firms have taken and then presents evidence suggesting that these investments have had a good private return.

Among the programs that firms have implemented are the following:

- *Hardening of Facilities.* Most of the companies we interviewed have made substantial physical improvements in their facilities since 1995–1996. Improvements have included hardening loading docks; installing secure doors with magnetic passcard or numeric password protection; creating limited-access vaults for high-value components; and installing closed-circuit television cameras.

- *Personnel Screening.* Our interviews revealed that personnel screening and background checks are now standard procedure for new hires in high-tech industries. According to some security managers, screening has reduced the problem of persons fired from one company for theft hiring on at another company.

- *Inventory Reduction and Improved Inventory Controls.* Many companies have improved their inventory management processes and systems. While inventory reductions and improved controls are part of a larger movement in industry to reduce costs and improve management of supply chains, security managers in some firms have been able to use inventory control systems to provide greater visibility into inventory variances, and as a tool for helping to determine which variances are likely due to shrinkage, or employee theft.

- *More-Discreet Packaging.* A tactic that has met with reportedly mixed success is removal of the contents identity from merchandise packaging. Some security managers indicated that packaging changes typically were quickly spotted by high-tech thieves, and that any benefits of changes to packaging were somewhat temporary. Other managers indicated that when logos or other information identifying the contents as high-tech merchandise was removed from packaging, their theft losses fell rather dramatically and have stayed low.[1] In many of the companies we interviewed, this issue typically pits security managers against marketing departments, and marketing departments have often prevailed. In some cases, firms may receive favorable pricing or face other incentives to put a supplier's logo on packaging, which can conflict with security objectives.[2]

- *Use of "Preferred" Freight Companies.* A number of firms have increased their reliance on one shipper or a small number of shippers to improve their leverage regarding the handling of their merchandise. Some security managers indicated that this effort

---

[1] Many security managers saw logos and other labeling information as a "steal me" message to would-be thieves.

[2] For example, many computer manufacturers indicate on their packaging the type of microprocessor inside the computer.

has resulted in carriers being more responsive to their firms' security concerns.[3]

- *Private Investigations of Theft Incidents.* Many firms investigate high-tech thefts to collect information that can be turned over to law enforcement agencies. Security managers try to build reasonably complete cases that law enforcement organizations can use for prosecution.

In our survey of study participants, data on security investments were gathered for the 1996 and 1997 calendar years. Table 4.1 summarizes these data. The 18 firms that provided complete data represent about one-half of the volume of thefts reported in the complete sample of firms participating in TIRS. Firms provided numbers for their total security budgets in 1996 and 1997, along with the percentage of those dollars that went to high-tech hardware theft prevention. In 1997, the portion of the security budgets allocated to high-tech loss prevention was slightly higher than the total value of hardware losses for the same year and one-third of total firm losses. On average, about 45 percent of the total budget was used for security guards and 29 percent was used for detection and monitoring. The rest was spent on investigations (3 percent), background investigations (6 percent), capital asset hardening (5 percent), and other personnel costs (12 percent).

Table 4.1

Reductions in Theft Losses and Security Investments

	Year =1996	Year = 1997
Number of firms	18	18
Sum of total security budgets	$93,286,627	$117,987,045
Sum of reported thefts	$80,043,731	$21,606,368
Average company-reported loss	$4,446,874	$1,200,354
Standard error, reported loss	$2,543,712	$607,400

---

[3]There also are industry-level efforts to improve the security of cargo, including the Technology Asset Protection Association's guidelines for transportation security. These industry-level efforts appear to be placing even greater pressure on carriers to improve their security procedures.

These firms experienced dramatic declines in total theft losses during this time period. The total number of reported losses averaged $4.4 million in 1996 for a total of over $80 million. This figure then fell by nearly 75 percent over a one-year period, suggesting that aggregate industry losses could have been as high as $1 billion in 1996.[4] High-value incidents were especially reduced, as indicated by a decline in the standard error (the average deviation from the mean) from over $2.5 million in 1996 to about $660,000 in 1997. Although several aforementioned factors could account for this decline, including increased public law enforcement support and lower margins for many high-tech products, it is likely that more-effective private-sector security efforts played a significant role.

To test this proposition, we examined the correlation between the changes in theft loss experiences for individual firms with individual changes in the security budgets. We found that the correlation between the two was very high (–0.92). Regressions linking thefts with security investments suggested that the firms with the largest increases in security were the ones experiencing the largest declines in thefts.[5] Although these simple correlations do not demonstrate causality, they are consistent with the hypothesis that security expenditures have paid off handsomely in the past and remain a solid investment for the future. Empirical findings suggest that security investments can return over a dollar in reduced losses for every dollar spent. Since this cost comparison does not consider any of the indirect savings enjoyed by the firm, industry, or consumers, it seems that higher investments may be warranted in the future.

---

[4]Under the assumption that industry thefts occurred at an annual rate of $250 million in 1997, a 75 percent decline since 1996 would imply an industry total of $1 billion in 1996. A couple of very-high-value incidents in 1996 accounted for almost one-third of the drop by 1997. When one removes these "influential outliers," the average decline falls to 50 percent. If one wishes to be more conservative, it would be reasonable to conclude that aggregate thefts fell between 50 and 74 percent between 1996 and 1998.

[5]The regression model specified the natural log of the ratio of hardware thefts, log(1997 losses)/log(1996 losses), as a function of the natural log of the ratio of security investments, log(1997 security/1996 security). The R-square was .472 and the estimated elasticity was –7.22 with a standard error of 2.32. Evaluated at 1997 averages, this implies that a 1 percent increase in the average budget (1 percent of $7.9 million = $79,000) would result in a 7.22 percent decline in thefts, or $86,000. Since it is unlikely that all of the increase in security expenditures is due to high-tech theft prevention, this calculation understates the return.

Chapter Five

SUMMARY OF FINDINGS AND POLICY CONCLUSIONS

In this final chapter, we summarize our main findings and draw policy conclusions from the perspective of individual firms, the industry, and the public sector.

SUMMARY OF FINDINGS

The findings of our study can be summarized as follows:

- Based on data provided by 95 firms representing approximately 40 percent of industry revenues derived from the manufacture and distribution of computers, semiconductors, hard disk drives, and cellular telephones, the estimated annual hardware loss amounts to almost $250 million. Even though these losses, expressed as a percentage of industry value added, are compounded as they are experienced along the chain of production and distribution, they still represent little more than 0.1 percent of industry revenues.

- The hardware losses of individual firms appear to vary predictably with market conditions. On average, losses are almost directly proportional to the total cost of goods sold. However, losses for high-margin firms (and, by implication, high-margin products) are much higher. High-end products, such as workstations, are also more likely to be stolen, holding other factors constant. This suggests that new, state-of-the-art products in high demand are particularly vulnerable.

- Direct losses may seem trivial, but, on average, they represent only the tip of the iceberg. Indirect costs, which include expensive theft-reduction strategies, lost sales, and other market adjustments, can dwarf direct costs. For the products most likely to be the preferred targets of thieves, these other costs can be as high as eight or nine times the direct hardware costs. Although precise estimates are not possible, we believe that these indirect costs of thefts from manufacturers and distributors can total over $1 billion.

- In addition to thefts from high-tech hardware firms, products stolen from customers can have a large impact on the bottom line of manufacturers. If customers anticipate theft probabilities, reductions in their willingness to pay for the vulnerable products will have important consequences for manufacturers. In fact, the economic impact of units stolen from customers is similar to that of units stolen from the high-tech producer.

- On the basis of the incidence of theft from the corporate and administrative offices of our sample firms, we estimate that $4 billion is stolen from the U.S. high-tech industry as a whole. This dollar figure may understate the problem, however, since it excludes theft from foreign operations as well as property stolen from nonbusiness customers.[1]

- In sum, these direct plus indirect losses exceed $5 billion, representing about 2 percent of industry revenues and a much higher percentage of net income. And it is important to note that we have not even considered losses from retail outlets or the potentially significant second-order effects associated with business disruptions and loss of valuable data or work product. These effects, which may be particularly pronounced for computers taken from business locations nationwide, could dramatically inflate the measure of economic costs, many of which would be passed on to the high-tech industries.

- When stolen product flows into markets served by victimized firms, these firms and their competitors suffer large losses because of displaced sales. These losses are only partially borne by

---

[1]It is important to note that this estimate is subject to greater uncertainty than our estimates of hardware losses directly incurred by high-tech product manufacturers. To the extent that other industrial sectors (i.e., business customers) experience different theft rates outside of corporate offices, our estimate will be inaccurate.

the firm actually experiencing the hardware theft: the smaller the market share of the victimized firm, the smaller its portion of displaced sales. This "externality" (i.e., costs being borne by market participants other than the theft victim) creates a disincentive to invest in activities designed to prevent losses industrywide.

- In response to the increased costs of doing business (due to security investments and anticipated hardware losses), firms change the prices at which they sell product and buy components. As a result, their suppliers and consumers bear a portion of the total costs of theft. In many situations likely to prevail in the high-tech industries we studied, these costs of doing business are considerable and can exceed the size of the direct cost by a multiple of two or three. These cost "pass-ons" can be viewed as another case of externality.

- External costs—those borne by the competitors, suppliers, and customers of the victimized firms—can represent a significant portion of the total costs of high-tech hardware theft. Depending on the underlying technological and market circumstances, they can range from 40 to 75 percent of the total.

- We found that total direct hardware losses have fallen dramatically since 1996. Based on survey data, the decline may have been as much as 75 percent and was no less than 50 percent. This decline may be partially due to changing market conditions, such as increased competition and lower margins in the relevant industries. Successful interventions on the part of the public law enforcement community may have also played a role. In addition, many firms made significant investments in private security measures over this time period. Although causation is hard to establish, firms that increased their security budgets the most over this period also experienced the greatest declines in hardware losses. The data are certainly consistent with the conclusion that these security investments had very high returns.

POLICY CONCLUSIONS

Policy Implications for Firms

Even though hardware losses represent a small slice of industry revenues, the indirect consequences of these thefts are significantly greater. The costs associated with lost sales and thefts at the customer level are in the vicinity of $5 billion. Considering the second-order effects, the overall magnitude of the problem warrants considerable attention on the part of high-tech manufacturers and distributors.

Our data suggest that firms have responded to this threat by investing in a variety of security measures that appear to have had a significant impact on total loss value. As recently as 1996, hardware losses were between two and three times higher than they were in 1998. Several factors may have contributed to this decline, including declining profit margins, greater competition, and more-effective law enforcement on the part of the public sector. At the same time, private security expenditures grew by 26 percent in one year alone. Our analysis indicates that the firms with the largest security budget increases were, on average, the ones that experienced the largest declines in thefts. Firms appear to be receiving more than a dollar-for-dollar return on their security investments, since these cost-benefit calculations do not consider the all-important second-order and indirect costs of theft. On average, it is reasonable to conclude that continued investments would be prudent.

We saw several patterns in the hardware losses reported by manufacturers. First, much of the lost value occurs when goods are in transit. In addition, thieves are much more likely to target firms that have high price-cost margins, reflecting products that are high end, state of the art, and in high demand. These two factors suggest that the highest security payoffs may lie in being better able to anticipate which products will be future targets of theft and in directing efforts at preventing in-transit losses of the products most attractive to thieves.

We believe that the following sorts of actions are warranted:

- *Focusing on the security of U.S. and European operations.* These two regions are the largest markets and account for the largest shares of theft.

- *Addressing the problem of in-transit theft.* In-transit theft is the most prevalent theft scenario, and effective action would staunch the flow of goods stolen while in transit.

- *Enhancing coordination within the firm.* Firms that have not already done so would probably benefit from increasing the exchange and coordination of information about theft problems and prevention. For example, a standing committee, including representatives from security, risk management, inventory management, production, distribution, transportation, and other relevant parts of the company, could facilitate data sharing on the changing patterns of losses.

- *Improving the ability to track the high-tech theft problem.* Firms should invest in processes and systems that improve their ability to collect and integrate theft-related information from security, inventory management, transportation, and other sources, and that provide a complete overview of the sources of losses (in-transit theft, shrinkage, etc.). This might be greatly facilitated by the creation of a standing committee (described in the previous bullet).

- *Improving the ability to anticipate changes in theft.* Changes in the marketplace are an important determinant of which products become sought after by thieves. Among the market factors that need to be considered are short-term shortages of new and improved products, and changing market shares. Firms might consider security investment strategies that differentiate on the basis of product or that change over a product's life cycle.

- *Targeting measures to the most-vulnerable products.* Consistent with the last paragraph, firms might improve the effectiveness of their interventions by targeting additional resources to their most vulnerable products, which typically will be their highest-value products. Product-specific cost-effective options should be explored to determine where best to spend additional security dollars.

- *Exploring other cost-effective options.* Our analysis suggests that the costs to firms of high-tech hardware theft are much higher than the simple cost of replacing stolen hardware. Because these costs are higher, options once rejected on the basis of cost-effectiveness may in fact be worthy of additional security resources. Firms should consider reevaluating some of these options in light of our findings.

Finally, the magnitude of losses stemming from the theft of final products from customers may be significantly greater than that for hardware taken directly from manufacturers. Although direct security measures will remain the primary responsibility of their business customers, manufacturers might contribute to theft reduction by developing technologies to render products inoperable when they are stolen, such as the "poison cookies" that disable products obtained illegally.

Policy Implications for Industry

We have seen that a significant portion of the indirect costs stemming from hardware theft is incurred by firms other than the firm experiencing the theft. This is primarily because displaced sales affect both the victimized firm and its competitors. In addition, the burden of hardware losses is partially passed on to suppliers. The existence of these external costs means that firms are not always willing to assume the cost of security measures when many of the benefits of doing so (in the form of reduced theft losses) will be partially reaped by other companies. Although firms may not have incentives to invest more in security on an *individual* basis, market participants could *collectively* improve their lot by putting more resources into theft-reducing measures. This suggests that industry-wide security efforts would pay off for all companies.

Estimates of theft losses to industry can only be improved if industry efforts to collect data on hardware theft losses not only continue but are broadened as well. Continued data collection will reveal which products become more or less vulnerable as the high-tech markets change, making possible early and decisive collective industry action to address these changes.

Currently, a number of industry activities promote higher levels of security awareness and develop joint solutions to the problem of high-tech hardware theft. For example, the Technology Asset Protection Association (TAPA) is an industry collaborative focusing attention on the development of shipping standards. A consortium of disk drive manufacturers is sharing information on individual members' theft experiences. These efforts illustrate the types of collaborative activities to date.

It is likely that further investments in industry standards and other cooperative policies could also benefit all firms. For example, individual firms may be unwilling to act independently with respect to the servicing of stolen product, but industry standards for this practice might be collectively beneficial. And industry cooperation on the development, standardization, and implementation of technologies that can identify and disable stolen products could well be the best approach to reducing losses stemming from thefts from the facilities of business customers.

Finally, during our interviews, several firms cited counterfeiting, remarking, and warranty fraud as increasing problems for high-tech manufacturers. These crimes are related to the direct theft of hardware, because much of the raw material for these activities is stolen. Currently, there is a dearth of information about the magnitude and implications of these emerging crimes. Industry collaboration for the collection and dissemination of information on these and other forms of crime would be an important first step.

Policy Implications for Society

In the accounting of total costs of theft, we found that a significant portion of the indirect costs is borne by customers of high-tech hardware producers. These losses, which actually exceed the replacement value of the hardware stolen, represent significant costs to society at large and serve to diminish the economic well-being of businesses and consumers across the nation and abroad. Manufacturers of computers, semiconductors, hard disk drives, and cellular telephones cannot be expected to consider the welfare of these other businesses and individuals in devising their individual strategies for combating high-tech hardware theft.

These considerations suggest that there is a role for the public sector. Some steps have already been taken. For example, California SB 1734 has been adopted and will provide $1 million to fight high-tech crime, a portion of which (10 percent) will go toward gathering more complete data on the problem. The State of New Jersey now requires localities to report all cargo thefts. These are good but isolated first steps. Society could well benefit from additional efforts that facilitate information exchanges between industry and law enforcement agencies and that increase collaboration in tracking the threat, anticipating the most likely future targets, and combining resources to mount an even more effective campaign against high-tech hardware thieves.

OVERVIEW OF THEFT INCIDENT REPORTING SYSTEM (TIRS) AND DATA COLLECTION PROTOCOLS

The Theft Incident Reporting System (TIRS) focuses on individual incident-level reporting of thefts. Participating companies were asked to provide the date, value of loss, and other information describing the stolen product and the circumstances of each theft incident. Following is an overview of recruitment and participation, and the data that we sought from participating firms.

RECRUITMENT, PARTICIPATION, AND VALIDATION

We began by inviting 500 firms in the computer, semiconductor, hard disk drive, and cellular telephone industries to access and use TIRS to report on theft incidents. We hypothesized that the total theft losses for each firm in each industry were likely to be associated with the firm's market share, essentially hypothesizing that the more product a firm produced, the greater its exposure to risk. Accordingly, the sampling frame was constructed by first selecting with certainty the largest 25 or so firms in each industry, and then selecting with a lower probability smaller firms in each industry. To maximize participation by firms selected with certainty, extensive follow-up efforts by mail and phone were made by RAND staff and project sponsors. This resulted in the agreement of 100 firms, concentrated among the largest in each industry, to participate in the TIRS data collection effort (though corporate mergers and subsequent attrition reduced the number of participants to 95).

For nine months, from October 1997 through June 1998, participating firms entered data describing their theft experiences into TIRS. After each quarter, we undertook an audit of theft reporting in the previous quarter. The audit consisted of asking each firm to check a RAND-prepared list of each theft incident reported, as well as aggregate summaries of various kinds, and to supply missing data wherever possible. For each firm, we sought to establish that (a) data for all of the incidents in the preceding quarter had been entered, and (b) data for the preceding quarter was accurate and complete.

Near the end of the study, all of the participating firms were asked to respond to a final questionnaire developed with the assistance of several companies that reviewed and pretested early drafts. These data were used, first, as a final consistency check on theft reporting from TIRS-participating companies; we asked each firm to report its total theft experience during the period of the study. The questionnaire also asked firms to provide data on their theft experience in earlier years so that we could estimate the percentage of their total theft experience they believed was captured in TIRS, and to provide additional information on warranty fraud, counterfeiting and re-marking, security spending, inventory controls, insurance, and other issues that had emerged in our case studies as being potentially important to understanding the full costs of high-tech hardware theft. We also again contacted some of the larger firms that had earlier declined to participate, to see if they would be willing to respond to the one-time questionnaire requesting aggregate information. In this way, we were able to supplement the TIRS data with additional aggregate data from firms that had not participated in TIRS.

THE THEFT INCIDENT REPORTING SYSTEM DATA COLLECTION INSTRUMENT

The TIRS data collection instrument consisted of an Incident Report and a Merchandise Report.

Incident Report Variables and Codes

The Incident Report was designed to capture basic descriptive information about each theft incident. Table A.1 provides information on the coding options that were available for three key incident-level variables: geographic location, scenario type, and location in the manufacturing cycle:

- The Date variables fix in time when the incident occurred, either as a discrete date or a range of dates if the exact date is unknown;

- The Total Value of Loss variable provides a single estimate of the total loss value;

- The Geographic Locations variables fix the location of the incident in broad geographic terms;

- The Incident Scenario Types variables identify the character of the theft incident in terms of type of crime;

- The Locations in Manufacturing Cycle variables aim to fix the location of the incident in the supply, manufacturing, and distribution chain.

MERCHANDISE REPORT VARIABLES AND CODES

For each theft incident, participating firms were asked to identify one or more types of merchandise that were targeted. Table A.2 provides a list of the merchandise codes that were available to participating firms.[1] For each type of merchandise identified as a target of theft in an incident, firms were asked to fill out a Merchandise Report that asked them to identify the quantity and value of each type of stolen merchandise, as well as who owned the merchandise, the purpose of the merchandise, and whether any recoveries had been made.

OPERATIONS

The TIRS instrument was available in paper-and-pencil format and electronically via Internet access to a privacy-protected dedicated server at RAND. Standard logic and data checking routines were applied to the database before and after downloading to analysis files.

---

[1] Readers will note that although the project generally focused on products within the computer equipment and cellular telephone industry, firms had the option of reporting on other types of high-tech equipment., e.g., telecommunications networking equipment, such as LAN routers.

Table A.1

Other TIRS Codes for Theft Incidents

DATE(S)
TOTAL VALUE OF LOSS
GEOGRAPHIC LOCATIONS
  US/City/State
  Other western hemisphere/City/Country
  Europe/City/Country
  Asia/City/Country
  Between locations (if in transit)
  Other (please describe):
  Unknown
INCIDENT SCENARIO TYPES
  Armed robbery (property taken by force)
  Attempted armed robbery
  Burglary (break-in & illegal removal of property)
  Attempted burglary
  Hijacking
  Attempted hijacking
  Theft (illegal removal of property without break-in or force)
  Attempted theft
  Shrinkage/inventory not accounted for
  Other (please describe):
  Unknown
LOCATIONS IN MANUFACTURING CYCLE
  On property occupied by your company
    Manufacturing or assembly area
    Warehousing/inventory storage area
    Loading/distribution/traffic area
    Corporate/administration area
    Other (please describe):
    Unknown
  Subcontractor facility
  In transit
    Airport
      Air cargo facility
      Carrier name
      Airport customs facility
      Other (please describe):
      Unknown
    At other customs facility
    Freight forwarder (please give name):
      On truck
      At facility
      Other (please describe):
      Unknown
  Other (please describe):
  Unknown

Table A.2

Merchandise Code List

Computers and desktop network file servers
    00 Microcomputer/PCs
    01 Laptop/notebook/palmtop PCs
    02 Desktop workstations
    03 Desktop network file servers
    04 Other computers
    05 Other network file servers
Magnetic disk storage devices and their components, and other computer peripherals
    10 Computer disk storage devices
    11 Microcontrollers or other semiconductors for magnetic disk storage devices
    12 Other electronic components for disk storage devices
    13 Other computer peripherals (e.g., monitors, keyboards, mouse, speakers,
        CD-ROMs)
Cellular telephones/PCS and components
    20 Handheld cellular telephones or personal communication systems (PCS)
    21 Flash memory for cellular/PCS
    22 Other semiconductors for cellular telephones/PCS
    23 Other electronic components for cellular telephones
Computer components
    30 CPUs (logic ICs) for computers or network file servers
    31 Memory ICs for computers or network file servers
    32 Other semiconductors for computers or network file servers
    33 Mother boards for computers or network file servers (i.e., boards populated
        with logic ICs)
    34 Memory boards for computers or network file servers (i.e., boards populated
        with memory ICs)
    35 Other populated boards for computers or network file servers (e.g., graphics
        boards, audio processing boards)
    36 Other electronic components for computers or network file servers
Other final products
    40 Other final products (please specify)
Other components
    50 Semiconductors for other final products
    51 Populated boards for other final products
    52 Other subassemblies or intermediate products for other final products
    53 Other electronic components for other final products
    60 Rejected components, not fit for use/sale
    61 Scrap material

TIRS provides an operating prototype for collecting standardized incident-level data for industry and subindustry monitoring of patterns and trends in thefts. Nonetheless, participation in this data collection activity placed added burdens on staff of security divisions, many of whom could not report complete information for their incidents. In some cases, project staff downloaded data from companies' custom information systems and transformed it into TIRS incident reports. The TIRS instrument could be significantly streamlined in the future to promote its ongoing use by firms in monitoring theft losses.

CASE STUDY PROTOCOL

A case study component was added to the study to help project analysts refine estimates of merchandise losses; estimate indirect losses associated with the theft problem; and assess prevention and other policy options that individual firms have employed. The case studies provided us with important information on "hidden" losses, "indirect" costs, and the benefits and costs of various theft reduction initiatives. The case studies involved a series of interviews (combining phone and in-person visits) with nine participating firms representing different industry sectors. These interviews focused on (1) placing thefts that companies reported in the context of their supply chains, customers, etc.; (2) obtaining insights into whether TIRS was obtaining a relatively complete record of theft losses in all parts of the company, or whether there were "hidden" losses (those not reported in TIRS) that should also be taken into account in estimating total losses; (3) understanding indirect costs of theft to firms, including line stoppages that result from shortages of stolen components, repairs to property, impacts of theft on other corporate operations; (4) identifying and assessing initiatives to reduce theft losses or their consequences that had been tried, were in place, or were under consideration, and their estimated costs; and (5) understanding better the size of nontheft losses attributable to counterfeiting, remarking and warranty fraud. Table A.3 summarizes the topics included in case study interviews with security and other representatives of selected firms. Subsequent to the case studies, the final audit questionnaire was developed to solicit similar input from the larger group of TIRS participants that received this questionnaire in the mail.

Table A.3

Interview Topics for Case Studies

- Overview of Company Operations (e.g., revenues, facility locations, products, supply and value chain, customers, freight forwarders)
- Security (e.g., overview of asset management and security programs and their estimated costs, typical responses to losses, inventory controls, estimates of losses not reported in TIRS, indirect costs, warrantee fraud, counterfeiting)
- Inventory Management (e.g., estimated inventory variances, losses by location, amount attributable to shrinkage/theft, etc., thresholds for reporting to security, inventory system coverage, capabilities, cost)
- Warrantee Claims and Counterfeiting (e.g., fraudulent claims, counterfeiting, re-markings, estimated losses, reporting thresholds, programs to reduce problem, including costs)
- Receiving/Materials Processing (e.g., estimated losses from theft/shrinkage, reporting thresholds, programs to reduce problem, including costs)
- Manufacturing/Assembly (e.g., estimated losses from theft/shrinkage, reporting thresholds, frequency of disruptions, percentage attributable to theft, cost of disruptions, programs to reduce problem, including costs)
- Warehousing (e.g., estimated losses from theft/shrinkage, reporting thresholds, programs to reduce problem, including costs)
- Distribution (e.g., estimated losses from theft/shrinkage, reporting thresholds, programs to reduce problem, including costs)
- Transportation (e.g., estimated losses, reporting thresholds, main freight forwarders, variance in theft experience by hauler, programs to reduce problem, including costs)
- Reclamation (e.g., estimated losses due to theft of rejected parts and waste that might be reclaimed, reporting thresholds, programs to reduce problem, including costs)
- Marketing (e.g., estimated market share for selected products)
- Customer Fulfillment (e.g., delays in customer fulfillment, programs to reduce problem, including costs, how much product replaced at zero cost?)
- Contracts (e.g., penalties for delays in delivery, costs of highly reliable suppliers, programs to reduce problem, including costs)
- Insurance (e.g., theft-related coverages, premiums, claims, payments, programs to reduce problem, including costs)
- Finance (review of financial report, e.g., U.S. vs. int'l sales by major product, line items of financial report that would include theft losses, sensitivity of R&D funding to margins, estimated market share for selected products)

MODELS OF THE INDIRECT COSTS OF THEFT

In this appendix, we present the underlying microeconomic models that form the basis for our simulations of the indirect economic costs borne by the victimized firm, the rest of the industry, and consumers when high-tech hardware is stolen. We present results from alternative economic models as well as a range of parameters so that we can evaluate the sensitivity of conclusions to our assumptions.

For all our simulations, we assume that demand for the product is given by a linear relationship between price and the quantities made available to customers either through normal sales channels or through gray or black market activities. Since we are interested in computing the ratios of different categories of indirect costs, not the absolute levels, these linearity approximations are reasonable. This is especially true given that, in reality, total thefts represent a small fraction of total output. Thus, demand is given by:

$$(1) \quad p = 100 - q_i - \eta t_i - \sum_{j=1}^{n}(q_j + \eta t_i)$$

where p is market price,

q_i is the quantity sold by firm i

t_i is the quantity of theft from firm i,

η is the degree of demand displacement (between 0 and 1),

q_j is the quantity sold by firm j,

t_j is the quantity of theft from firm j, and

n represents the number of competitors.

The degree of demand displacement reflects the degree to which stolen property is viewed as being substitutable for product purchased through normal channels. In this characterization, we are not explicitly differentiating between consumers who acquire stolen product and those who continue to make purchases from legitimate sources only.[1]

For our first set of simulations, we assume that the amount of theft depends on the quantity of output sold as well as the firm's investment in security. In alternative models outlined below, we explicitly model the behavior of thieves and derive alternative relationships between theft and security investments. The quantity of theft is given by:

$$(2) \quad t_i = q_i \big/ s_i$$

That is, the amount stolen, t_i, increases with the quantity sold and is inversely correlated with the units of security investments, s_i. The units of security represent different activities, such as increased use of guards, asset production equipment, or inventory control processes. All firms (n of them) are assumed to face identical relationships.

Costs of production for firm i are given by:

$$(3) \quad C_i = m(q_i + t_i) + s_i^2 + \gamma s_i q_i$$

where m represents the marginal cost of production,

s_i^2 represents the fixed cost of investing in security and

γ represents the degree to which marginal costs of production are increased due to security investments (varies between 0 and 1).

---

[1]We have also explored models in which we model separate consumer groups. Even in cases where those purchasing stolen property through gray market channels at lower prices would not have purchased hardware through normal channels (because, for example, prices were too high), our general conclusions are not materially affected. That is, the lost welfare (due to higher prices) suffered by traditional customers and victimized firms is invariably greater than the benefits accruing to those acquiring stolen property at lower prices.

Equations (1) through (3) can be combined to obtain an expression for firm profits given by:

$$(4) \quad \Pi_i = [100 - (q_i - {}^{\eta q_j}\!\!/_{s_j})]q_i - m({}^{q_i}\!\!/_{s_i}) - s_i^2 - \gamma s_i q_i$$

Firm i will act to maximize profit with respect to quantity and levels of security. Using a standard Cournot model, we assume that the firm will select optimal levels of output and security under the assumption that the levels chosen by each of the n competitors remain constant. Assuming n homogeneous competitors implies that quantities and levels of security chosen will be the same for all firms. This yields the following first-order conditions:

$$(5) \quad {}^{\delta \Pi_i}\!\!/_{\delta q_i} + 100 - 2q_i - 2\eta q_i\big/_{s_i} - \sum_{j=1}^{n}(q_j + {}^{\eta q_j}\!\!/_{s_j}) - m - {}^{m}\!\!/_{s_i} - \gamma s_i = 0$$

$$\text{or } q_i = \frac{[100 - m - m\big/s_i - \gamma s_i]}{[(2 + n)(1 + \eta/s_i)]}$$

$$(6) \quad {}^{\delta \Pi_i}\!\!/_{\delta s_i} = {}^{\eta q_i^2}\!\!/_{s_i^2} + {}^{m q_i}\!\!/_{s_i^2} - 2s_i - \gamma q_i = 0$$

This model was used to simulate market outcomes and relationships between hardware losses and indirect costs, including investments in security, lost sales to the firm and its competitors, and declines in consumer welfare. Outcomes were compared for different underlying assumptions concerning the marginal cost of replacement (m), the degree of competition in the industry (n), the degree to which sales are displaced by stolen product (η), and the degree to which security investments increase the marginal cost of production (γ). Results from this simulation are provided in Table B.1. The entries include simulated outcomes for quantities, price, security investments, hardware thefts, and a measure of consumer surplus given by

$$(7) \quad C_{si} = .5(n + 1)(q_i + \eta t_i)^2$$

It is important to note that this expression includes the value of stolen goods received by customers. To the extent that final customers are aware (or at least suspect) that these goods are stolen, counting these stolen goods as contributing to social welfare may understate the total losses associated with hardware theft.

In Table B.2, loss ratios are calculated showing the magnitude of losses in comparison with direct measures of hardware losses. For example, for the first row, the firm will lose 1.6 times the total hardware cost (in terms of lost profits). From Table B.1, profit falls to 414.6 (from 625.0) following the theft of $134.0 of hardware valued at replacement cost (m times quantity stolen). Consumer surplus falls by over $80, primarily because prices rise to 78.1 from 75.

The entry under the heading "industry sales" represents the decline in firm-level profits that stems from displaced sales due to thefts from other firms in the industry. When $n = 0$ (there are no other firms) or when there is no sales displacement, these losses are zero. In contrast, when $n = 4$ and there is full sales displacement (the tenth entry from the top), each firm suffers a total loss of 0.3 (as a fraction of hardware losses). These losses are already included in total firm loss ratios.

The last column represents the percentage of total industry losses that is external—i.e., imposed on market participants other than the firm directly suffering the initial hardware loss. External losses include losses to consumers as well as those due to industry sales displacement. In the reported simulations, these range from 11 percent to as high as 72 percent. In many scenarios, most of the burden of theft is not incurred by the firm in the best position to prevent theft through investments in security. Rather, it is borne by consumers and other firms in the industry.

To further test the sensitivity of these results to alternative model assumptions, we explored alternative model characterizations. In general, our qualitative results were relatively invariant. For example, we can assume that the activity of thieves is modeled as a competitive fringe that is responsive to prevailing market prices. That is, thieves will steal product as long as the marginal cost of doing so is exceeded by the market price at which they can sell (fence) the stolen goods. Say that the marginal cost of stealing from a particular firm i is positively related to the quantity of goods

Table B.1

Simulations

Parameters				Quantity q_i	Security s_i	Thefts t_i	Price p	Total Costs	Profit Π	Consumer Surplus	Hardware Theft	Security Cost
n	η	γ	m									
0	0	0	50	25.0	0.0	0.0	75.0	1250.0	625.0	312.5	0.0	0.0
0	0	0	50	21.9	8.2	2.7	78.1	1298.4	414.6	240.8	134.0	67.0
0	0	1	50	17.7	5.5	3.2	82.3	1174.7	283.2	157.0	159.8	129.0
0	1	0	50	19.9	8.9	2.2	77.8	1187.6	363.5	246.0	112.4	78.6
0	1	1	50	15.3	6.0	2.5	82.2	1021.0	236.6	159.2	126.7	129.0
0	0.5	0.5	50	18.3	6.9	2.7	80.4	1159.1	312.5	193.0	133.2	110.3
4	0	0	50	8.3	0.0	0.0	58.3	416.7	69.4	173.6	0.0	0.0
4	0	0	50	6.8	5.5	1.2	65.8	433.9	15.9	116.7	61.6	30.8
4	0	1	50	5.7	4.4	1.3	71.4	395.1	13.0	81.6	64.5	44.9
4	1	0	50	5.7	5.4	1.1	66.0	369.4	9.6	115.5	52.9	29.5
4	1	1	50	4.6	4.4	1.1	71.5	323.8	7.4	81.1	53.2	39.1
4	0.5	0.5	50	5.6	4.9	1.2	68.9	377.2	11.3	96.6	57.9	37.4
0	0	0	20	40.0	0.0	0.0	60.0	800.0	1600.0	800.0	0.0	0.0
0	0	0	20	38.6	7.3	5.3	61.4	931.7	1439.0	746.0	106.1	53.0
0	0	1	20	35.5	4.0	8.8	64.5	1045.6	1244.3	630.3	175.9	159.6
0	1	0	20	35.4	9.9	3.6	61.0	878.7	1282.7	760.3	71.3	98.8
0	1	1	20	30.3	6.0	5.0	64.7	924.4	1034.1	624.2	100.9	217.8
0	0.5	0.5	20	34.2	6.5	5.3	63.2	942.6	1217.8	678.5	105.3	153.2

Table B.1—continued

Parameters				Quantity q_i	Security s_i	Thefts t_i	Price p	Total Costs	Profit Π	Consumer Hardware		Security Cost
n	η	γ	m							Surplus	Theft	
4	0	0	20	13.3	0.0	0.0	33.3	266.7	177.8	444.4	0.0	0.0
4	0	0	20	12.7	5.0	2.5	36.7	329.1	135.3	401.3	50.5	25.2
4	0	1	20	11.8	3.5	3.3	41.0	357.0	126.8	348.2	66.7	54.2
4	1	0	20	10.8	5.5	2.0	36.4	284.7	106.9	404.9	39.2	30.2
4	1	1	20	9.5	4.0	2.4	40.8	290.5	96.0	350.1	47.4	53.8
4	0.5	0.5	20	11.0	4.4	2.5	38.9	312.8	114.4	372.8	49.7	43.8
1	0	0	10	30.0	0.0	0.0	40.0	300.0	900.0	900.0	0.0	0.0
1	0	0	10	29.4	5.3	5.6	41.3	377.2	834.7	862.5	55.7	27.8
1	0	1	10	27.9	2.9	9.7	44.2	464.2	769.1	777.4	96.8	88.6
1	1	0	10	26.2	7.8	3.4	40.9	356.6	714.3	874.5	33.6	60.8
1	1	1	10	22.9	4.8	4.8	44.6	410.7	612.3	767.4	47.6	133.7
1	0.5	0.5	10	25.9	5.1	5.1	43.0	402.1	713.5	812.1	51.1	91.6

Table B.2

Loss Ratios

Parameter				Ratio to Direct Theft				Percent External
n	η	γ	m	Lost Profits	Industry Sales	Consumer Surplus	Total Cost	
0	0	0	50	1.6	0.0	0.5	2.1	25%
0	0	1	50	2.1	0.0	1.0	3.1	31%
0	1	0	50	2.3	0.0	0.6	2.9	20%
0	1	1	50	3.1	0.0	1.2	4.3	28%
0	0.5	0.5	50	2.3	0.0	0.9	3.2	28%
4	0	0	50	0.9	0.0	0.9	1.8	52%
4	0	1	50	0.9	0.3	1.4	2.3	62%
4	1	0	50	1.1	0.3	1.1	2.2	61%
4	1	1	50	1.2	0.3	1.7	2.9	69%
4	0.5	0.5	50	1.0	0.1	1.3	2.3	63%
0	0	0	20	1.5	0.0	0.5	2.0	25%
0	0	1	20	2.0	0.0	1.0	3.0	32%
0	1	0	20	4.5	0.0	0.6	5.0	11%
0	1	1	20	5.6	0.0	1.7	7.3	24%
0	0.5	0.5	20	3.6	0.0	1.2	4.8	24%
4	0	0	20	0.8	0.0	0.9	1.7	50%
4	0	1	20	0.8	0.0	1.4	2.2	65%
4	1	0	20	1.8	0.7	1.0	2.8	59%
4	1	1	20	1.7	0.7	2.0	3.7	72%
4	0.5	0.5	20	1.3	0.3	1.4	2.7	65%
1	0	0	10	1.2	0.0	0.7	1.8	36%
1	0	1	10	1.4	0.0	1.3	2.6	48%
1	1	0	10	5.5	1.5	0.8	6.3	37%
1	1	1	10	6.0	1.5	2.8	8.8	48%
1	0.5	0.5	10	3.6	0.8	1.7	5.4	46%

sold, q_i, and inversely related to the firm's investment in security, s_i. Specifically, assume that the marginal cost of theft is given by

(8) $MC(t) = s_i t_i / q_i$

Since thieves will steal up to the point where $p = MC$, we can derive a new expression for theft:

(9) $t_i = p q_i / s_i$

That is, theft will be a function of the total revenue of the firm, not simply the units of output, as in the previous formulation. Substituting the expression for theft into the demand function yields a new expression for price:

$$(10) \quad p = \left(100 - q_i - \sum_{j=1}^{n} q_j\right) s_i \Big/ \left[s_i + \eta q_i + \eta s_i \sum_{j=1}^{n} q_j / s_j\right]$$

Now, assume costs of production are given by:

$$(11) \quad C_i = m(q_i + t_i) + \gamma s_i^2 / 25 + (1 - \gamma) s_i q_i / 25$$

where *m* represents the marginal cost of production,

$s_i^2/25$ represents the fixed cost of investing in security and
γ represents the degree to which marginal costs of production are increased due to security investments (varies between 0 and 1).

With substitution for t_i and some rearranging, we get the following expression for profit:

$$\Pi i = \frac{\left(100 - q_i - \sum_{j=1}^{n} q_j\right) q_i (s_i - m)}{\left[s_i + \eta q_i + \eta s_i \sum_{j=1}^{n} q_j / s_j\right]} - m q_i - \gamma s_i^2 / 25 - (1 - \gamma) s_i q_i / 25$$

Taking the derivative with respect to q_i yields the following first-order condition:

$$(12)\ \delta\Pi_i / \delta q_i = -\eta(s_i - m)(100 - q_i - \sum_{j=1}^{n} q_j)q_i/[s_i + \eta q_i + s_i\sum_{j=1}^{n} q_j / s_j]^2$$

$$+[(100 - 2q_i - \sum_{j=1}^{n} q_j)(s_i - m)]/[s_i + \eta q_i + \eta s_i\sum_{j=1}^{n} q_j / s_j]$$

$$-m - (1 - \gamma)s_i / 25 = 0$$

Recall that all firms are identical, which means that the sums of industry q and industry s are $(n+1)q_i$ and $(n+1)s_i$, respectively. Next, taking the derivative with respect to s_i yields the second condition for maximizing profits:

$$(13)\ \ \delta\Pi_i / \delta s_i = -(s_i - m)(100 - q_i$$

$$-\sum_{j=1}^{n} q_j)q_i(1 + \eta\sum_{j=1}^{n} q_j / s_i)\bigg/ [s_i + \eta q_i + \eta s_i\sum_{j=1}^{n} q_j / s_j]^2$$

$$+(100 - q_i - \sum_{j=1}^{n} q_j)q_i\bigg/ [s_i + \eta q_i + \eta s_i\sum_{j=1}^{n} q_j / s_j]$$

$$-2\gamma s_i / 25 - (1 - \gamma)q_i / 25$$

These first-order conditions can be used to derive equilibrium levels of prices, quantities produced, theft, profits, security costs, and consumer surplus as a function of market parameters. Qualitatively, the results for these simulations were similar to those reported in Table B.1. In general, however, firms bear a higher portion of the total cost of theft since they are less able to pass cost increases on to consumers. This is because increases in prices will induce higher theft rates. In general, consumer surplus losses were about half the magnitude of those discussed earlier.

Finally, we demonstrate that theft from final consumers can have an impact similar to that of theft directly from manufacturers. To illustrate, imagine that a single firm faces the following demand curve:

(14) $P = 100 - q$

Costs are equal to mq where m represents marginal costs.

(15) $\Pi = (100 - q)q - mq$

Now, imagine that final consumers expect to lose t percent of q to theft.

As a result, the implicit price of the good becomes $p(1 + t)$ and demand can now be expressed as

(16) $(1 + t)p = 100 - q$ or $p = (100 - q)/(1 + t)$

since firms earn revenue of p for goods sold, q, as well as for those that are stolen.

Thus, the profit function becomes

(17) $\Pi = \left[(100 - q)\bigg/(1 + t) \right][q(1 + t)] - (1 + t)mq$

Maximizing profit with respect to q yields

(18) $\delta\Pi\big/\delta q = 100 - 2q - (1 + t)m = 0$

This outcome is identical to that obtained via a t percent rise in the marginal cost of production. In other words, the market outcome and the incidence of theft are identical to those obtained when the same degree of theft is experienced at the manufacturing source. From the perspective of both the manufacturer and final consumer, both outcomes are identical.

STATISTICAL ANALYSIS OF LOSS PATTERNS

In this appendix, we present the details of our econometric analysis of direct losses. Our model related the reported theft loss (in natural logarithms) to a set of explanatory variables, including the cost of goods sold (in logarithms), the net income (as a percentage of revenue), and the percentage of total revenues accounted for by sales of workstations, semiconductors, hard drives, and cellular telephones. The estimates are reported in Table C.1.

The model R-squared of .403 indicates that the included variables explain about 40 percent of the variation in losses. The coefficient estimate for the effect of the cost of goods sold demonstrates that expected losses expand nearly in direct proportion to the total volume of wholesale value, all things held equal. The estimated effect of net income is also positive and significant. The estimates indicate that for a firm earning margins that are 20 percentage points higher than those of another firm (as in the case of microprocessors versus hard disk drives), expected losses would normally be 76 percent higher (the coefficient of 3.844 times the margin difference of .20). Since new, state-of-the-art products can have margins that are even higher, the loss experience could be three or four times higher for products that are in the greatest demand.

The estimates also indicate that high-end equipment is especially vulnerable. Workstation producers suffer losses triple those of lower-end PC producers, holding other factors constant. Hard drive producers also suffer higher losses. Cellular phones and semiconductor producers have lower theft rates. Other models that included quarterly indicator variables indicate that seasonal effects are not pronounced when seasonal variation in revenues is controlled for. Most systematic variations are due to typical fluctuations in sales and net income, which have a seasonal pattern.

Table C.1

Statistical Analysis of Hardware Losses

Dependent variable: log (theft loss)	Coefficient	Standard Error
Independent variables:		
Intercept	4.733**	2.009
log(cost of goods sold)	0.940*	0.238
Net income (percent of revenue)	3.844**	1.921
Workstation revenues (percent of total)	1.957**	0.923
Hard drive revenues (percent of total)	1.674	0.933
Cellular phone revenues (percent of total)	0.573	2.091
Semiconductor revenues (percent of total)	0.463	0.834
R-Squared = .403		
**Significant at 95%		
*Significant at 99%		

NOTE: Only 54 observations had complete information for this analysis. Only 30 percent of firms report losses for any given quarter. This reflects the low volume of business for the small firms in the sample. In addition, market share measures were difficult to obtain for many firms.

BIBLIOGRAPHY

American Electronics Association, "High-Tech Industry Leads the Nation in Driving the U.S. Economy," press release, November 18, 1997.

Bazeley, Michael, "Tech Firm Robbed by Trio; Chips Likely Target in Fremont Holdup," *San Jose Mercury News*, March 23, 1998, p. 5B.

Benner, Lamar, *The Computer Industry, 1997/98 Edition*, Dun & Bradstreet, 1997.

Bermayer, Joel B., "Information Highway Robbery: High-Tech Heists, as BellSouth Learned, Are a Growth Industry," *Raleigh News and Observer*, January 11, 1998.

California Assembly Committee on Public Safety, "Computer Crime: Challenges to Industry, Law Enforcement and the Legislature," informational hearing, September 30, 1997.

California Highway Patrol, "Cargo Theft Summary Data for the Period," August 1998.

Coalition Against Insurance Fraud, "Estimated Nationwide Claims Fraud, 1994," <http://www.insurancefraud.org/94_est.htm>.

Coalition Against Insurance Fraud, "Insurance Fraud: The Hidden Tax," <http://www.insurancefraud.org/facts.html>.

"An EBN Extra: 1998 Top Semiconductor Suppliers," *Electronic Buyers' News*, March 30, 1998.

Freeh, Louis J., statement as delivered by Louis J. Freeh, Director, Federal Bureau of Investigation, before the Senate Select Committee on Intelligence and Senate Committee on the Judiciary, Subcommittee on Terrorism, Technology and Government Information, Hearing on Economic Espionage, February 28, 1996.

Goodfriend, B. Dale, and Barry J. Wilkins, "Study of Best Asset Management Practices in the Computer Industry," BJSI.

Hayward, Douglas, "IBM Pilots Free Chip—Theft Deterrence Service," *TechWeb News*, October 21, 1997.

"High Tech Thieves Head to Greener Pastures: Europe," *EETimes*, May 22, 1996.

Information Technology Industry Council (ITI), *Information Technology Industry Data Book, 1998–2008*, Washington, D.C.: ITI, 1998.

Kane, Margaret, "IBM: Can it Regain Its Luster?" *ZD Network News*, August 4, 1998, <http://www.zdnet.com/zdnn/>.

Liotta, Bettyann, "Knogo Strip—On Chips," *Electronic Buyers' News*, December 11, 1995.

Mello, John P., Jr., "Stop Thief: While Hackers Get the Headlines, Computer Hardware Thieves Have Quietly Become an Expensive Headache," *CFO Magazine*, October 1997.

Semiconductor Industry Association, *World Semiconductor Trade Statistics (WSTS)*, global billings report history.

Microcomputer Statistics Committee, Information Technology Industry Council, "Microcomputer Unit Shipments in the United States," August 1998.

Owens, Charles L., statement of Charles L. Owens, Chief, Financial Crimes Section, Federal Bureau of Investigation, before the U.S. House of Representatives Committee on Ways and Means, Subcommittee on Health, Washington, D.C., October 9, 1997.

Robertson, Jack, "Counterfeit Pentiums Seized—Groups in Europe, Asia Linked to Re-Marked ICs," *Electronic Buyers' News*, December 9, 1996.

Safeware Insurance, "$2.3 Billion in Computers Lost During 1996," press release, February 14, 1997.

Safeware Insurance, "Columbus, Ohio—More Than 1.5 Million Computers Were Stolen, Damaged or Otherwise Destroyed During 1997," <http://www.safeware-ins.com/losses97.html>.

Sargent, Matt, "Retail Desktop Sales for June: Compaq Bounces Back with Strong Sales of Win98 Systems, IBM Jumps to No. 2 in Retail Desktop Sales," Aaron Goldberg's Infobead Insider, July 28, 1998, <http://www.ci.infobeads.com/Insider/>, 1998.

Sargent, Matt, "Intel Sees a Bull on the Horizon: Q3 Revenues Are Looking Good," Aaron Goldbert's Infobead Insider, September 11, 1998, <http://www.ci.infobeads.com/Insider/>, 1998.

Standard and Poor's, *Telecommunications: Wireless*, Industry Survey, June 25, 1998, p. 3.

U.S. Department of Justice, *Sourcebook of Criminal Justice Statistics 1996*, Washington, D.C.: U.S. Government Printing Office, 1997.

U.S. Department of Justice, Federal Bureau of Investigation, *Crime in the United States 1996*, Washington, D.C.: U.S. Government Printing Office, September 28, 1997.

U.S. Department of Justice, Federal Bureau of Investigation, *Uniform Crime Reports; 1997 Preliminary Annual Release*, May 17, 1998.

Wallace, Bill, "15 Indicted in Bay Area Microchip Robbery," *San Francisco Chronicle*, May 21, 1998.